101 Reasons
to Dump Your Man
and Get a Cat

101 Reasons
to Dump Your Man
and Get a Cat

Molly Katz *(yeah, really)*

WILLIAM MORROW
An Imprint of HarperCollinsPublishers

HarperCollins books may be purchased for educational, business, or sales promotional use. For information please write: Special Markets Department, HarperCollins Publishers, 10 East 53rd Street, New York, NY 10022.

FIRST EDITION

Designed by Nicola Ferguson
Illustrations © 2006 by Merle Nacht

Library of Congress Cataloging-in-Publication Data

Katz, Molly.
    101 reasons to dump your man and get a cat/Molly Katz; illustrations by Merle Nacht.
        p. cm.
    ISBN 13: 978-0-06-088474-1
    ISBN 10: 0-06-088474-6
    1. Man-woman relationships. 2. Cats. I. Title: 101 reasons to dump your man and get a cat. II. Title.

HQ801.K354 2006
306.7—dc22

2005057498

06 07 08 09 10 ❖/TOPPAN 10 9 8 7 6 5 4 3 2 1

For Buddy,
who never says he'll call
and then doesn't

— Molly Katz

For Arthur

—Merle Nacht

Acknowledgments

Thanks so much to

Henry Morrison and

Sarah Durand

For your vision and enthusiasm

And to

Tom and Sherry Koski

For Buddy

In the Litter Box
of Relationships,
Shit Happens

Well, the relationship news is worse than ever. Nobody's into anybody, and everybody is searching for somebody.

Statisticians tell us the number of happy human couples is dropping faster than they can count. Ecstatic marriage counselors are buying Prada briefcases and limited-edition Ferraris. To get an appointment with a counselor, at least one member of the couple must be in intensive care.

The shocking figures were revealed in a recent nationwide poll. Four million people responded to the following questions:

Do you love your spouse/partner?

No: 94%

Yes: 3%

Don't Know: 3%

Most Frequent Comment: "I know I love my cat."

Would you rescue your spouse/partner if he or she was about to get eaten by a bear?

No: 89%

Yes: 5%

Don't Know: 6%

Most Frequent Comment: "Maybe, once I made sure the cat was indoors."

· Would you divorce your spouse and marry your cat if you could?

No: 1%

Yes: 99%

Most Frequent Comment: "Where can I buy a really small ring?"

· How long have you been with your spouse/partner?

Too Long: 39%

Way Too Long: 61%

Most Frequent Comment: "I have no idea. But I've had my cat for six years, two months, and five cherished days."

- Does your spouse/partner ever threaten to leave?

  No: 8%

  No, Damn It: 92%

  Most Frequent Comment: "Fine with me, as long as he/she doesn't try to take the cat."

- What is your primary household expenditure?

  Rent: 4%

  Transportation: 2%

  Little Fuzzy Squeaky Toys: 94%

- What is your spouse/partner's most irritating habit?

  Lying: 4%

Stealing: 3%

Buying Stupid Healthy Cat Food Instead of What Tastes Good to the Cat: 93%

· How many cats does it take to screw in a lightbulb?

Don't Know: 2%

Don't Care: 3%

I Would Never Bother My Precious Cat with Such a Menial Chore: 95%

Husbands and boyfriends I've had, you don't want to know how many. They—excuse the expression—come and go. But my cat, Buddy, ain't goin' nowhere.

Buddy is a beautiful tuxedo with a delicious soft coat and an irresistible baritone purr. He does have his flaws. Buddy likes to lie down any time I do. "Lie down" means to fight me for every bit of couch or bed space, but slowly, so I don't notice until I realize my body is frozen, hanging at the edge of the furniture. He believes any food I'm working with is for him, including meat, eggs, butter, soup, salad, or substances that smell like food, such as lip balm or shampoo. He insists on being included in every activity—making the bed, doing the laundry, taking a shower, throwing a party, writing. You wouldn't believe what four cat feet on a keyboard can do.

But I never have to fight Buddy for the car keys when he's had too many mai tais. He doesn't head for the litter box carrying a newspaper. And I know he won't cheat on me with his baby mama.

've never had a man whose fur
I could bury my face in when
I was sad.

So, to the bottom line . . .
Cats *are* the ideal species
preference if one is to cohabit.

And here's why . . .

When you're packing to go away,
your man won't climb into your
suitcase and refuse to get out.

You don't have to take your cat-in-law to dinner on Mother's Day.

You don't need to panic over how to tell your cat your period is late.

You can talk for hours on the phone without pissing off your cat.

No one has ever been stood up
by a cat.

Your cat's parents won't pressure you to convert to their religion.

Your man can't scratch his ear
with his foot.

here are no cat lawyers.

ou can't make the bed with your man in it, and then giggle at the little lump.

Your cat doesn't care if you
have an innocent little drink
with your boss.

ats *expect* love at first sight.

A man can't use his whiskers to tell if his body will fit somewhere.

ou don't need to call four of your girlfriends to analyze what your cat said.

Cats hunt alone, not out with
the guys.

your music, always.

Your man doesn't have pink toes
and black toes on the same foot.

Your cat's feelings won't be hurt
if you never put on the lilac garter
belt he gave you.

If your cat is attracted to the cat sitter, so what?

Cats are supposed to
sneak around
go out alone
have back hair

If your man poops on the rug,
there's a much bigger problem.

ou never have to remind your cat
to use deodorant.

No man can entertain himself
all morning with one rubber band.

Your cat really can hang from the chandelier.

Your cat won't hang a stuffed
mouse head on the wall.

Your man won't get rid of the bugs
in the house by eating them.

Your cat doesn't have to compare
his penis with other cats'.

Your man can't stretch his body to twice its normal length.

Cats *never* have difficulty
showing emotion.

When you step on your man's foot, you can't pick him up and make it all right with a nuzzle.

Cats don't go to the grocery store and come back with marinated elk hooves but no toilet paper.

Hair balls, not hairy balls.

You don't have to stand on your tiptoes to kiss your cat.

Your mother will never nag you about which cat to marry.

our man can't come and go as he pleases through his own little square in the back door.

You don't have to pretend
to your cat that you haven't had
many other cats.

You don't get to call your man affectionate nicknames like "Skunk Face" and "Pork Sandwich."

Two words:
one dish.

You never have to worry about whether it's okay to date your cat's ex.

Your cat doesn't scatter the contents of his pockets on the dresser every night.

Your cat doesn't take his wiener in his paw and shake it after peeing.

You won't find suspicious numbers on your cat's cell phone.

Cats never notice
when you have
a new zit.

You don't have to convince your cat to wear a condom, or pretend to like putting it on for him.

Your man's fur doesn't smell
sweetly of spit.

ou won't find a copy of
Lick-a-licious Poontang
magazine in your cat's desk.

ou don't need to care if your friends don't like your cat.

Your cat won't get transferred
to Pittsburgh.

It wouldn't be adorable if your man pounced off the fridge onto your shoulder.

Your parents won't push you to give them grandcats.

our cat's fly is never open.

When a cat thinks he's doing something charming, he is.

Cats don't have to put on a
silly suit and hat and drive
somewhere to play ball.

You don't have to worry about insulting your guests if your cat nods off during their visit.

our man can't confer on you the honor of a silky paw to caress.

You'd worry if your man left little nibble marks on your plants.

Your cat will never use your toothbrush.

ou won't get arrested if you have
your cat castrated.

ou never have to worry that your
cat thinks your friends are hot.

Your cat will never tell you
he loves you but
he's not *in* love with you.

You don't need to lose five pounds
before getting naked with your cat
the first time.

You don't have to pretend size doesn't matter.

137

Cats don't take up a lot of
closet space.

Your cat doesn't leave pee drips
all around the litter box.

our man won't wake you by licking your face with his tiny, spiny pink tongue.

You never have to remember how your cat takes his coffee.

Your cat doesn't care
if you keep the light on
when he's trying to sleep.

You won't need to yell at
your cat for changing lanes
without signaling.

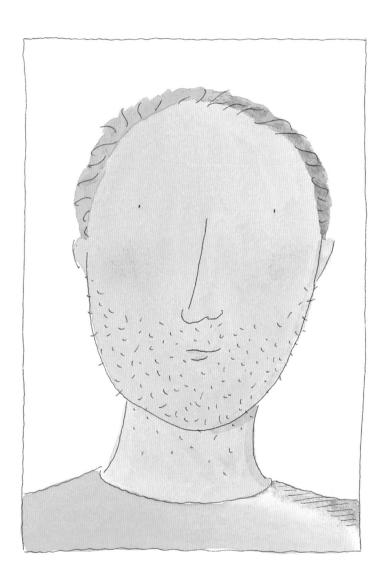

Long, soft whiskers.

Your man won't amuse you by selecting the most flattering plants among which to pose prettily.

Cats don't come home from the gym and make you feel their quads.

ou never have to watch your cat arranging a scarf around his neck, and wonder if he really is straight.

You can't improve your man's mood by tossing a fuzzy mousie for him to chase.

Your cat doesn't throw up
his paws and ask other cats what
women want.

You'd hate it if your man insisted
on keeping you company
in the bathroom.

Your cat doesn't comb his
hair eight different ways to hide
the bald spot.

You won't get to watch your man climb up the inside of the Christmas tree and bat the ornaments around.

Cat hobbies aren't expensive.

ou never have to fake it.

Cats don't try to kiss you
in the morning before they've
brushed their teeth.

ou never have to see your cat
in a Speedo.

Cats don't BlackBerry you in
the middle of your pedicure.

No need to explain the importance of foreplay.

Cats don't have midlife crises and
go out and buy motorcycles.

You don't have to laugh at your cat's jokes.

Lap dances are fun for *you*.

our cat won't get into bed naked
with his socks on.

our cat won't insist he's three inches taller than he really is.

Your cat won't flirt with other cats on the computer.

our cat won't stumble home
hammered and want to make love.

.

Cats don't pretend to know what region the wine comes from.

ou can't use your fingertip
to stroke your man's little fuzzy
wet nose.

Cats understand that farts aren't hilarious.

ou can't have more than one man.

ou can't watch your man sleep
in a patch of sun on the floor.

There's only so much pillow
a cat can hog.

Your cat doesn't care how much older you are.

our cat gets clean without leaving a wet towel on the floor.

You don't get to watch your man
nudge aside another man
to eat his food.

ou don't have to beat yourself up
for sleeping with the wrong cat.

Your cat won't admit he's wrong either, but at least he doesn't keep you up all night trying to prove he's right.

our man can't crouch in a paper bag with only his whiskers sticking out, twinkling in the sun.